COACHES
ENCOURAGE
BOSSES
PUNISH

4 Secrets To Perfect Coaching, Perfect Supervising, Perfect Parenting And Building Successful And Lasting Relationships.

GORDON JACKSON

COACHES ENCOURAGE BOSSES PUNISH

All inquires should be to:

Professional Resources Center, Inc.
P. O. Box 382036
Memphis, TN 38183-2036

Library of Congress Cataloging – in – Publication Data

Jackson, Gordon, 1939 -

COACHES ENCOURAGE – BOSSES PUNISH – Four Secrets to Perfect Coaching, Perfect Supervision, Perfect Parenting and Building Successful and Lasting Relationships.

ISBN 0-9673304-0-8

Coaches Encourage – Bosses Punish

Dedication

This book is dedicated to my
beloved wife, Sandy, who provides
me with the gift of encouragement
every moment of my life and
positively reinforces the goodness
in everyone she meets.

Coaches Encourage – Bosses Punish

Acknowledgments

To those who provide me an opportunity to encourage and reinforce their positive behaviors.

Angela, Celeste, Eric and Amanda – my dear children.

Alex, Peyton, Carson, Josh and Chandler – my darling grandchildren.

To those who continue to positively reinforce my each and every new "project":

Carol Gatlin – my administrative assistant, who worked diligently through at least ten drafts of the manuscript to this book.

Steve Shields, Ted Yeiser and Frank Cantrell – fellow partners at Jackson, Shields, Yeiser and Cantrell whose support provides me the opportunity to complete such projects as *COACHES ENCOURAGE – BOSSES PUNISH.*

All members and staff of Jackson, Shields, Yeiser And Cantrell whose cooperative spirits make it a pleasure to be part of their team.

To those who supply me a lifetime laboratory to study the powers of positive reinforcement:

Wayne Jackson, Bobby Jackson, Martha Barnes, Jimmy Jackson, Gary Jackson and Carlette Hardin – my siblings.

And, of course, to my parents:

Carl and Cora Jackson – who "encouraged my heart" each and every day of their life.

Table of Contents

COACHES ENCOURAGE – BOSSES PUNISH

is a book for all seasons in that it provides a timeless resource to build the best of all types of relationships.

Preface

Whenever a child observes a parent approaching, the child looks upon the parent in one of two ways: the parent is there to encourage or the parent is there to punish.

Whenever an employee observes a manager approaching, the employee looks upon the manager in one of two ways: the manager is there to encourage or the manager is there to punish.

COACHES ENCOURAGE – BOSSES PUNISH outlines a process through which to build successful and lasting relationships between management and employees by providing to employees the "gift of encouragement" and utilizing the "power of positive reinforcement."

COACHES ENCOURAGE – BOSSES PUNISH defines a process through which to build effective and enduring relationships of all types, whether between parent and child, husband and wife, teacher and student, business associates, friends or, of course, coaches to players, simply by encouraging and reinforcing the positive behavior of the other.

As a management consultant, author and speaker, specializing in positive employee relations, I have observed a revolution in the American workplace during the past 30 years.

This revolution in the American workplace has occurred because effective managers, supervisors and leaders have come to understand that a punitive approach to supervision is not the answer to achieving peak performance and building positive employee relations. Effective managers, supervisors and leaders now understand that peak performance and effective and enduring relationships are products of reinforced positive behaviors.

The revolution in the workplace has occurred as a result of a mindset change on the part of managers, supervisors and leaders from that of the "Punisher of the Past" to the "Encourager of the Future"; from that of the "Boss of the Past" to the "Coach of the Future."

As a parent and as a grandparent, I also have observed during the past 30 years a parallel revolution in the American family. This revolution has occurred as a result of a paradigm shift on the part of the parent from that of the "Punisher of the Past" to the "Encourager of the Future."

Unfortunately, the revolution of the "Punisher of the Past" to the "Encourager" has not been completed.

In many homes, the parental approach continues to be a punitive one, even during the nurturing years when the child is unaware of what truly is expected of him or her. In some workplaces, the preferred management approach continues to be a punitive one, even when the employee is being trained.

The punitive approach appears to be the standard applied in too many of all types of relationships. The coach punishes the player for "missing a basket." The wife punishes the husband for a failure to remember their anniversary date. The husband punishes the wife because of the headache. A friend punishes a neighbor for not having been invited to a party.

Irrespective of the positive approaches to building effective and enduring relationships through the application of "encouragement," there yet are so many who have failed to understand and appreciate the magic associated with "positive reinforcement."

Hopefully, the "Four Secrets to Perfect Coaching, Perfect Supervising, Perfect Parenting, and Building Successful and Lasting Relationships," as discussed in this book, will help complete the revolution from the "Punisher of the Past" to the "Encourager of the Future."

COACHES ENCOURAGE – BOSSES PUNISH is dedicated to the completion of this change in that it is a book for all seasons. It provides a timeless resource to build the best of all types of relationships.

COACHES ENCOURAGE – BOSSES PUNISH is not intended to pronounce some "quick fix" to achieve effective relationships. Rather, its purpose is to identify and refine some basic universal truths and timeless principles, when sequenced correctly, can be used to build the best, most successful, and longest lasting relationships, whether at work, on the playing field, in the classroom, or in the home.

The term "Perfect," as used in the subtitle of this book, is one of degree and relevance. The term "Perfect" is intended to convey a process by which to build the best relationships possible, given the strengths and weaknesses of those who are parties to the relationship and the particular circumstances associated with the relationship.

The term "Perfect" to a coach should be interpreted to mean that applying the "Four Secrets" will build the best relationship he or she can develop with a given player. It means that the "best" coach may be the coach who takes a challenged player and develops such player to his or her maximum ability by applying the "Four Secrets." It could mean, conversely, that a "worst" coach may be one who takes a highly talented player and destroys such talents by a failure to apply the "Four Secrets."

The term "Perfect" to a parent should be interpreted that by applying the "Four Secrets," he or she will have a better opportunity of developing the most effective relationship possible with a given child. It means that the "best" parent may be the parent who takes a challenged child and develops such child to his or her maximum abilities by using the "Four Secrets." Conversely, it could mean that a "worst" parent may be one who is blessed with a very gifted child and destroys the child's potential by a failure to apply the "Four Secrets."

The term "Perfect" to a manager, likewise, means to use the "Four Secrets" to develop and maximize the potential of all employees, associates and team members.

The "Four Secrets" are not intended to substitute for the basic essentials of any meaningful relationship.

Unless a manager truly cares for the employee under his or her supervision, the relationship is likely to suffer, irrespective of the application of the "Four Secrets." Unless a parent has unconditional love for his or her child, the relationship is limited, regardless of using the "Four Secrets."

Indeed, as Lou Holtz, the famous football coach and renowned professional speaker, often exclaims: *"Trust, Commitment* and *Love"* are the essential fundamentals of any successful relationship. In all types of relationships, "people don't care how much you know until they know how much you care."

Neither is *COACHES ENCOURAGE – BOSSES PUNISH* intended to convey that coaching, supervising and parenting are simple tasks. They are most complex. It is intended to share a process through which coaching, supervising and parenting can be less complex.

COACHES ENCOURAGE – BOSSES PUNISH, likewise, is not intended to suggest that building other types of relationships are simple processes. All types of relationships present their own uniqueness and challenges.

It is intended to suggest a failure to apply any one or more of the "Four Secrets" to any type of relationship is to create a vacuum in the relationship, the consequence of which could cause the relationship to be less successful than otherwise. It is intended to suggest that a failure to apply any of the "Four Secrets" may carve a hole so deep into the "soul" of the relationship, that the relationship is doomed from the beginning.

Had the "Four Secrets" been understood, appreciated and applied in the twentieth century, society may have suffered fewer wars, fewer prisons, fewer mental institutions, fewer divorces, and fewer dysfunctional families and individuals.

If society should have learned one lesson in its transition through the twentieth century – and the centuries before it – the lesson is that *punishment cannot be used as a means to train or nurture others.* In that sense, punishment destroys relationships. But, on the other hand, when "encouragement" and "positive reinforcement" are used as training and nurturing tools, the best, most successful and longest lasting relationships can be built.

Who are the very best in giving "encouragement" and "reinforcing" positive behaviors?

In Florence Littauer's "must read" book, entitled, *Silver Boxes* and subtitled, *The Gift Of Encouragement*, it was her father who "encouraged" her to achieve great accomplishments and success as one of the most profound professional speakers in the speaking industry.

In your life, it may have been that one coach, that one teacher, that one friend, that one parent, brother or sister, grandparent, godparent, or loved-one who encouraged you when you may have needed it most of all.

But, I truly believe it is the mothers of this world who best provide the "gift of encouragement" and supply the "power of positive reinforcement," day-in/day-out.

As a professional speaker, my mother had always hinted that if and when I were to speak in my hometown, she would like to be invited as a guest.

I had never encouraged such an invitation even when I was in her geographical "neck of the woods" until a few years ago when I was invited to present the keynote address for an Association's Annual Convention in Nashville, Tennessee.

Given the fact my mother resided merely 20 miles north of Nashville and that my speech – *How To Motivate People* – was going to be presented in a 40 minute time slot, I thought it a perfect occasion to invite her to attend.

The circumstances worked out quite well because one of my brothers was in a position to bring my mother to the hotel while I was putting some last-minute touches on my presentation.

The convention was "kicked-off" by the program director. Shortly thereafter, I was introduced and, in turn, I introduced my mother and younger brother who were sitting "down-front" in the meeting room.

As I was coming to some concluding comments in my presentation, I glanced down at my mother and realized that I should include her in some way in my closing remarks.

But how, I pondered?

I then thought to myself: I know what I can do. I can conclude with some comments from Stephen Covey's *The Seven Habits Of Highly Effective People.*

Stephen Covey frequently asks, "What is the purpose of life?" He then explains the true purpose of life is *to live, to love, to learn* but, most significantly, *to leave a legacy.*

I remarked to those in the audience that most of us will not leave a legacy when we depart this earth in terms of great wealth. On the other hand, the one legacy all of us can leave behind is to reflect back on our lives and say, "I encouraged a lot of people."

I concluded my remarks by suggesting to the audience that any applause they may have reserved for me that morning, to please direct their applause to someone who had been encouraging others for more than 80 years, including 7 children, 15 grandchildren, and so many great-grandchildren it was difficult to keep up with them anymore. Then pointing in the direction of my mother, I almost shouted: **"MY MOMMA!!"**

In more than 30 years of professional speaking, the only truly deserving standing ovation I may have ever received from an audience was that very morning and, even then, the standing ovation was not for me. It was for – **MY MOMMA!**

Here's to you and to those with whom you want to build a successful relationship and a lasting legacy.

Gordon Jackson

The best, most successful and longest lasting relationships are built upon two dynamics:

The Impact of Encouragement and the Power of Positive Reinforcement.

1

The
First
Secret

Coaches Encourage – Bosses Punish

1.
The First Secret

The number one criticism by American employees of American management is that "You don't define expectations; you don't let us know what you expect of us."

The same criticism applies to the American family. Parents do not define expectations for their children. They do not inform their children what they expect of them.

The same criticism applies in spousal and other types of relationships. Neither party to the relationship informs the other of their expectations. Too often, it all becomes a "guessing game."

Why don't managers and leaders in the American workplace inform employees, associates and team members what they expect of them in terms of performance, quality, productivity, safety, and in terms of behavior; indeed, in terms of all their expectations?

How is it possible for employees to perform in accordance with their managers' expectations unless the managers inform such employees exactly what they expect of them? How is it possible for children to measure up to their parents' expectations unless the parents inform such children specifically what they expect of them?

How is it possible for team members to meet the expectations of their coaches unless the coaches inform the team members precisely what they expect of them?

Therefore, it should come as no surprise that the first universal principle necessary in building any type of successful and lasting relationship with another – whether spouse, child, player, student or employee – consists of two simple words: **DEFINE EXPECTATIONS.**

It may appear too simplistic to state, categorically, that the "First Secret" is to define the expectations one wishes the other to meet or exceed in a given relationship.

It, in fact, is too simplistic.

Indeed, the "First Secret" entails more than merely explaining to another what is expected. "Defining Expectation" requires an application of several specific disciplines.

DISCIPLINE NUMBER ONE

The first essential discipline is to define expectations only for those in the relationship who possess the requisite "ability" to meet or exceed such expectations.

Unless an employee has the potential "ability" to meet the expectations of the organization, defining such expectations for the employee is a futile exercise, irrespective of the amount of "encouragement" and "positive reinforcement."

Likewise, to define an expectation for a player beyond his or her "ability" to meet such expectation results in frustration and disappointment for the entire team.

The only way that
you can motivate
another person –
whether child,
employee, player,
friend, or loved-
one – is to provide
an environment or
basis by which
that person can
motivate himself
or herself!

Worst, perhaps, is to define expectations beyond the "ability" of a child, the consequence of which is a loss of self-esteem and dignity on the part of the child and a heightened level of frustration and disappointment on the part of the parent.

Therefore, it is a fundamental principle in relationship building to define expectations *only* for those in the relationship who have the ability to meet or exceed the expectations.

On the other hand, when expectations are defined for those who have the ability to meet the expectations, and a willingness to accept the challenge, a foundation then is established on which the individual can be *motivated*, to meet and, hopefully, exceed what is expected.

The age-old question is: "How do you motivate?"

For the parent: "How do I motivate my children?" For the teacher: "How do I motivate my students?" For the manager: "How do I motivate my employees?" For the coach: "How do I motivate my players?"

Motivate to do what? Motivate the other person in the relationship to meet or exceed your expectations of him or her.

But without a "Defined Expectation" by the parent of the child, by the teacher of the student, by the manager of the employee or by the coach of the player, there is no basis of motivation; there is nothing about which to be motivated.

The only way that you can motivate another person – whether child, employee, student, player, friend or loved-one – is to provide an environment or basis by and through which that person can motivate himself or herself.

"Defining expectations" for those who possess the "ability" to meet or exceed the expectation provides *that* basis and foundation of motivation. "Defining expectations" provides *that* environment by and through which the other person in the relationship can motivate himself or herself, intrinsically – from within.

Sometimes in my speaking endeavors, I am challenged about this proposition: that the best way to motivate another is to provide the other person with an environment by and through which he or she can be motivated from within.

When challenged, I merely relate a story that originated during World War II. A young Lieutenant was regaling the wonderment of a new GI insurance program to thousands of troops who were to be sent overseas. After an hour presentation about the new GI insurance, the young Lieutenant asked for a showing of hands of those who might be interested. No one raised their hands. The Lieutenant was dejected until an old Sergeant raised his hand and asked permission to say a few words to the troops. The Lieutenant nodded, affirmatively.

The old Sergeant took the microphone and announced that within the week, they all would be sent overseas; that some of them would be sent to the "front lines" and, unfortunately, some of them would not be coming back.

He went on to say: "as the Lieutenant has already explained, for those who enroll in this new GI insurance and who are killed in the war, the U.S. Government will be obligated to send their family a check for $10,000. But for those who do not enroll in this new GI insurance and are killed in the war, the U.S. Government will not be obligated to send their family one single dime."

The old Sergeant hesitated, then calmly inquired;

"Who in the world do you believe the U.S. Government will be sending to the "front lines"; those who if enrolled in the new GI insurance and killed in the war, the U.S. Government will be obligated to send their family a check for $10,000 – or those, who if not enrolled in the new GI insurance and killed in the war, the U.S. Government will not be obligated to send their families one single dime?"

Its true: the best way to motivate another is to provide an environment in which the other person is motivated from within.

Please do not jump to a conclusion that external pressures or outside forces do not motivate. They do, but only to the extent that such external pressures or outside forces provide the other person an environment by which he or she will be motivated, from within.

DISCIPLINE NUMBER TWO

The second essential discipline applicable to "Defining Expectations" is to distinguish the difference between "Defining Expectations" and "Setting Goals."

Hopefully, we all set goals – for ourselves.

It somewhat is impossible, however, to set a goal for another person. It is not impossible, on the other hand, to define what we expect of another person.

The other person may accept and comply with what we define as our expectations of her or him, in which case, both parties then have mutual goals; otherwise, they remain "our goals."

There is no question but that "goal setting" is important for organizations, for parents, for coaches; indeed for all of us. But "goal setting" merely is the antecedent in terms of "Defining Expectations." Until the receiving party accepts the expectation as his or her own goal, the "expectational" loop is never closed.

It is *possible* for those who have the "ability" but who lack the "desire" to meet or exceed expectations; it is *impossible* for those who lack the "ability" but who have the "desire" to meet or exceed expectations.

DISCIPLINE NUMBER THREE

The third essential discipline associated with "Defining Expectations" is to appreciate the difference between "ability" and "desire."

When the term "ability" is used in connection with "Defining Expectations," it means the individual has the potential to meet or exceed the expectations, once properly trained.

Thus, "ability" in this context does not mean present or existing ability necessarily; rather, it means that the individual has the potential ability – the innate ability – to meet or exceed the expectations, once he or she is properly trained to do so.

The fact that it is the *potential* ability that is to be measured rather than the *present* ability, determining this *potential* ability might well require an assumption that one has the ability, initially. Thereafter, the second and third secrets can be used to validate whether or not he or she possesses the true ability to meet such expectations.

It is possible to determine some "defined abilities" at the inception. For example, if an employer requires an administrative employee to type at least 75 words per minute but a typing test of the applicant reveals that he or she can only type 40 words per minute, then the "potential" ability is not relevant.

On the other hand, an individual may possess the ability to meet the expectation but has no desire to meet the expectation.

For example, a child may have the "ability" to meet or exceed a parent's expectations but not the "desire." The child's ability is not an issue. But, because of a lack of desire, the child *may not* want to meet the expectations.

Similarly, an employee may have the "ability" to meet or exceed a manager's expectations of him or her, but not the "desire." The "ability" is not an issue. The employee *can*. The issue, again, is one of lack of desire. The employee *may not* want to meet such expectations.

It is *possible* for those who have the "ability" but who lack the "desire" to meet or exceed expectations; it is *impossible* for those who lack the "ability" but who have the "desire" to meet or exceed expectations.

Certainly, parents, coaches, and employers should provide every reasonable and feasible accommodation possible to ensure their respective child, player, or employee is given the opportunity to meet whatever the expectations. Such obligation, whether inherent or legally required, is presumed to have been applied for purposes of this discussion.

Whether one can meet the "Defined Expectations," with or without other accommodations, is the preliminary question that arises in the "First Secret." If the individual has the requisite "ability" to meet the expectation, the second question then is to determine whether the other person in the relationship has the "desire" to meet, or exceed, the expectation.

The ideal foundation for any management/employee, parent/child, coach/player or any other type of relationship is one in which the individual has both the "ability" and the "desire."

Although the ideal is to define expectations only for those who have both the "ability" and "desire" to meet or exceed such expectations, what is the solution to a situation in which the individual *can* meet the expectation but has no desire to do so?

Defining expectations is not a one-way street: the most effective and enduring relationships are built upon a mutuality of "Defining Expectations."

In such a circumstance, the question becomes: is it possible to motivate an individual who has the present "ability" to meet or exceed certain defined expectations, but not the present "desire?"

YES. But how?

By applying the "Second Secret to Perfect Coaching, Perfect Supervising, Perfect Parenting, and Building Successful and Lasting Relationships"; that is: by "Establishing Consequences."

Prior to discussing the "Second Secret," however, there are some additional disciplines that should be understood with regard to "Defining Expectations."

DISCIPLINE NUMBER FOUR

The fourth discipline associated with "Defining Expectations" is to appreciate that relationship building is not a one-way street. The most effective and enduring relationships are built upon a mutuality of "Defining Expectations."

One may have interpreted from the earlier discussion that the "First Secret" only is applicable to those relationships in which the person defining the expectations stands in some superior relationship to the other, such as a parent to a child, a teacher to a student, a manager to an employee, a coach to a player and so on.

Not so!

"Defining Expectations," at least in the context it is used in this book, is intended to be applied on a mutual basis and in a bilateral manner.

That means, an employee defines in his or her mind certain expectations of his or her manager; that a player defines in his or her mind certain expectations of his or her coach; that a child defines in his or her mind certain expectations of his or her parent.

Mutual expectations mean, also, that even a spouse or mate defines in her or his mind certain expectations of the other – and vice-versa.

Perhaps with the exception of a parent-child relationship, unconditional relationships can become very conditional in the absence of mutual contributions to the relationship and a failure to meet mutual expectations.

Equally significant, when mutual expectations are not defined in a realistic and achievable manner, one or both of those so defining expectations of the other will suffer disappointment, resulting in an unsuccessful relationship – in the long term.

For example, one could reasonably argue that the most successful marriages are those in which each spouse shares with his or her mate what is expected of the other.

Couples in explaining the reasons for a divorce typically blame the termination of the relationship on a "lack of communication." A more rational and honest explanation might be that one or both failed to convey what he or she expected of the other.

Although there may be some passing comment at the time of the divorce that he or she "did not meet my needs," rarely is there a true acknowledgment that "we failed to convey to one another what we truly wanted from the relationship; we simply did not share what we expected of each other."

Unless expectations are
defined in some way to
the other person in the
relationship, whether the
relationship is one of
friendship, family
or otherwise, the
relationship, over time,
will merely wither away,
without the other person
ever realizing why or even
having an opportunity to
attempt to make the
relationship work.

DISCIPLINE NUMBER FIVE

The fifth discipline relating to "Defining Expectations" requires a certain sensitivity in the manner an expectation should be defined.

Particularly, marital and social protocol might require a more diplomatic approach to defining what one expects in a given relationship.

Therefore, the earlier discussion about marriages was not meant to convey that each party to the relationship should tender an itemized list to the other of exactly what is expected of each other on the eve of the wedding. The "unconditional love" each has vowed to the other might become a little too "conditional" rather late in the game.

But, there may have been numerous occasions leading up to this point of the relationship where both general and specific expectations could have been conveyed, either expressly or implicitly, and in a diplomatic and civil manner. If such expectations were defined before marriages rather than afterwards, there might be fewer marriages. True. There, indeed, might be fewer divorces and fewer dysfunctional marriages as well.

In terms of applying diplomacy when "Defining Expectations" of others, no one likely is going to convey to a friend that "here are my expectations of you and if you can not meet these expectations, our friendship is history."

Most likely, these types of expectations are conveyed in more subtle tones and in more sensitive terms; more implicitly communicated rather than expressly stated. Unless expectations are defined in some way to the other person in the relationship, however, whether the relationship is one of friendship, family or otherwise, the relationship, over time, will merely wither away, without the other person ever realizing why or even having an opportunity to attempt to make the relationship work.

How many friendships eventually evaporate over time, without either party truly understanding the reason? Were the situation honestly assessed, the answer most likely would be a failure of each to have effectively expressed in some way what he or she expected of the other.

DISCIPLINE NUMBER SIX

The sixth discipline applicable to "Defining Expectations" is to appreciate the necessity to repeat and reinforce such expectations on an on-going basis.

It is important to revisit the age-old axiom: "Repetition is the mother of learning."

It also is important to realize that, typically, there are incremental expectations within any ultimate expectation. Likewise, some expectations are more important and significant than others. This suggests that more time and effort should be spent in terms of "defining" and "reinforcing" the most important and significant expectations and, perhaps, less time and effort should be devoted to matters of less importance.

A related dynamic associated with "Defining Expectations" is to appreciate that expectations of others, change, just as needs of individuals, change, both of which require even more communications relative to "re-defining" and "fine-tuning" expectations of others on an on-going basis.

In addition to the disciplines associated with the "First Secret" there also are certain time-tested axioms that should be considered when "Defining Expectations."

Some of these timeless axioms consist of the following:

1.

Expectations should be compatible with the ethics and values of both the person defining the expectations as well as the person for whom the expectations are being defined.

2.

Expectations should be communicated precisely and with sufficient clarity.

3.

Expectations should be stated in a positive manner. The subconscious processes positive thoughts much more readily than it processes negative thoughts.

4.

Expectations should be measurable so that accurate feedback can be provided to the individual responsible for meeting or exceeding the expectations.

5.

In most situations, expectations should have time lines by which to measure progress. Who, what, where, why and how are wonderful descriptive pronouns, but nothing happens until the "when" kicks in.

6.

Expectations should be defined in such a manner that the end result can be visualized.

7.

Expectations should be realistic and achievable.

8.

Expectations should be defined only by those who would be willing to perform such expectations, themselves, assuming they possessed the skills and abilities to do so.

Remember
a failure to "Define Expectations" creates a vacuum in the relationship, the consequence of which is likely to cause the relationship to be less successful than otherwise.

2

The Second Secret

Coaches Encourage – Bosses Punish

2.
The Second Secret

The "First Secret" establishes a foundation on which to build successful relationships.

Without "Defining Expectations," there is no basis or foundation upon which the other secrets can function. "Defining Expectations" is the antecedent to building any type of effective and enduring relationship.

But once expectations are defined, the other secrets sequentially follow – in a very simplistic manner.

The "Second Secret to Perfect Coaching, Perfect Supervising, Perfect Parenting, and Building Successful and Lasting Relationships" again, consists of two words: ESTABLISH CONSEQUENCES.

"Without consequences there will be no behavioral modification."

– Morris Massey

It is a universally recognized truth that few modify their behaviors unless consequences attach.

Perhaps better stated is to paraphrase the values-systems guru, Morris Massey: "Without consequences, there will be no behavioral modification."

THE IMPACT OF NEGATIVE CONSEQUENCES

The "Second Secret" dictates that both "negative consequences" as well as "positive consequences" be discussed with the individual responsible for meeting the expectations.

So many times, managers, coaches, teachers, and parents only want to discuss the "positive consequences" that will result if and when an employee, team member, student, or child behaves or performs in accordance with what is expected.

Isn't it "just so much fun" to talk about rewards and recognition – incentives, promotions, "goodies," etc. Isn't it just a "hoot" to embellish all the wonderful things that will happen if the child, the employee, the student, the player, or whomever, meets our expectations. It almost sounds crass to discuss the downside: what will happen if the individual fails to fulfill our expectations?

Given the proposition that the only way to motivate another is to provide an environment by and through which the individual will be motivated from within, establishing "negative consequences" may prove to be as beneficial as establishing "positive consequences."

For example, everyone seems to be intrigued by innovative methods of parenting. "Tough love" is a good example, although, admittedly not all that new or innovative.

Many children by the time they enter their teens are so out of control parents are told to engage in "tough love" with their child. The parents then enter into a "contract" that provides the child must meet certain conditions, or otherwise, he or she will no longer be permitted to remain in the home.

No one really knows the true success of the "tough love" approach, but the question has to be asked: why did the parents wait until the teenage years when the child was so out of control before applying the "First and Second Secrets"; that is, to "Define Expectations and Establish Consequences?"

THE DOCTRINE OF
ASSURED RESPONSE

During the "Cold War," the United States communicated to the Soviet Union exactly what would happen if the Soviet Union launched nuclear missiles toward American soil. The United States referred to its military position as what could be characterized as the "Doctrine of Assured Response."

The "Doctrine Of Assured Response" means that when one establishes a negative consequence for another he or she can be assured that such consequence will be exercised if expectations are not met.

What if the Soviet Union had not believed the United States intended to respond in such a manner?

Isn't it amusing that organizations fail to apply the "Doctrine of Assured Response" to applicants. So many are hesitant to inform applicants of the negative consequences that will apply if they do not measure up to the organization's standards?

Likewise, it is amusing to observe managements' failure to apply the "Doctrine of Assured Response" when faced with disciplinary decisions.

Were managers and supervisors to apply the "Doctrine Of Assured Response" in disciplinary actions, one might be less exposed to this common refrain in the American workplace:

"This is your *second* final warning."

and two weeks later:

"This is your *third* final warning."

and two weeks later:

"This is your *fourth* final warning."

and so on: The *fifth* final warning, the *sixth* final warning, the *seventh* final warning – *ad nauseam*.

Isn't it also amusing that parents, teachers, and coaches fail to apply the "Doctrine of Assured Response" to their respective children, students, and players when misbehaving.

If parents would apply the "Doctrine Of Assured Response," you and I might be spared this common refrain from parents to their misbehaving youngsters:

"If I have to warn you *just one more time*."

a few minutes later:

"If I have to warn you *just one more time*."

a few minutes later:

"You are trying my patience – just try me – *just one more time*.

and *just one more time; just one more time; just one more time – ad nauseam*.

Thank goodness the Soviet Union never found out about America's preoccupation with such phrases as the "**SECOND, THIRD, FOURTH, FIFTH, SIX** or **SEVENTH FINAL WARNING**" or "**JUST ONE MORE TIME**," during the cold war.

ESTABLISH
CONSEQUENCES EARLY

Another requirement associated with "Establishing Consequences" is that they should be addressed prior to the training or nurturing process, rather than afterwards.

Obviously, there are some behaviors so offensive that the consequences are presumed. Whether an organization has in its "Conduct Code" that stealing company products is a dischargeable offense, employees inferentially understand the consequences for such behavior.

But most expectations and corresponding consequences need more explanation.

Just as expectations must be defined before the expectations are to be met, consequences must be established before the consequences are to be addressed. "Defining Expectations" and "Establishing Consequences" should be addressed in a timely sequence, if not simultaneously.

ESTABLISHING CONSEQUENCES REQUIRES "DUE PROCESS"

Judicial "Due Process" means, among other things, that one is given advanced notice of some law, regulation or requirement before he or she can be held accountable for failing to comply with such.

Therefore, workplace "Due Process" means an employee should be informed in the beginning about what consequences will apply if she or he fails to perform or behave in keeping with the organization's policies.

Parental and coaching "Due Process" means that a child or player should be informed in the beginning about what consequences will occur if she or he does not meet the expectations.

Establishing "Positive Consequences" as well as establishing "Negative Consequences" can create an environment in which employees, team members, and children can motivate themselves from within.

Perhaps, it is my sensitivities to a lack of justice with regard to certain types of relationships. But, I become livid when observing a parent physically punishing a child over some behavior the child had no clue was inappropriate.

I equally become distressed when observing a supervisor reprimanding an employee over some behavioral or performance requirement about which the employee had no knowledge.

THE IMPACT OF
POSITIVE CONSEQUENCES

Once "Negative Consequences" are established and understood, it equally is important to establish "Positive Consequences" in the event expectations *are* met.

Just as with "Negative Consequences," when "Positive Consequences" are applied, they too can provide a basis for motivation – an environment in which one can motivate himself or herself, from within.

Parents, coaches, teachers, managers, and others who are responsible for building relationships should be sensitive when to emphasize "positive consequences" and when to emphasize "negative consequences."

Legendary coaches have long pronounced that with some players, it is necessary to stress "negative consequences" in order to motivate a given player to his or her maximum potential. While, on the other hand, with certain other players, reconfirming "positive consequences" creates a more productive climate.

RECOGNIZE, REINFORCE AND REWARD

There are numerous "positive consequences" that may apply to those who meet or exceed expectations.

First of all, when individuals meet, or exceed, what is expected of them, their behavior should be **Recognized, Reinforced** and **Rewarded**.

In terms of **Recognizing**, **Reinforcing** and **Rewarding** an individual for meeting or exceeding expectations, it is important to remember two basic maxims:

1.
Reward Only For Those Things You Wish To Achieve

"What get's rewarded get's done; what does not get rewarded doesn't get done," comments Michael LeBoeuf, author of the best selling book, GMP, an abbreviation for the "GREATEST MANAGEMENT PRINCIPLE."

In other words, reward only for those things you want to achieve. If you want to achieve more team spirit, then you should reward people for working together as a team, rather than rewarding for individual efforts.

2.
Recognize, Reinforce and Reward Only For Positive Behavior

Reward for negative behavior and you receive negative results. On the other hand,

and more positively stated, reward for positive behavior and you receive positive results. Positive reinforcement begets positive results.

Also, in terms of **Recognizing**, **Reinforcing** and **Rewarding** for positive results, it may be beneficial to appreciate that non-monetary reinforcers and rewards may produce more favorable results than do monetary rewards and reinforcers.

There is no denial that money motivates. Monetary bonuses, for example, have been used historically to reward and reinforce individuals who have met or exceeded expectations.

Monetary bonuses particularly are motivational for those whose income and resources supply only a meager standard of living for the human condition. For those who are more affluent, monetary bonuses may be motivational merely as a means of keeping "score" in comparison with peers who may be moving "up the ladder."

But there are some limitations associated with using money solely as a means to **Recognize**, **Reinforce** and **Reward** for positive results.

First of all, monetary bonuses easily can be interpreted as entitlements which, from an employee's perspective, may become a subconscious part of her or his pay and compensation. For example, sometimes it is an employer's intent that a certain defined monetary bonus be awarded for an exceptional year. Yet, employees may have interpreted such a bonus to be a standard practice for the future, whether an exceptional year or not, and conclude that the bonus is more than a gratuity. It is an entitlement.

The same example can be applied when rewarding children, players, or others in a relationship when money is used to the exclusion of non-monetary rewards and reinforcers.

THE "TROPHY EFFECT"

Children, players, students, and employees need to be rewarded with more than money to symbolize the positive consequences of having met or exceeded what is expected of them. They need a "trophy" in the form of something different from money to symbolize they have won.

Non-monetary reinforcers and rewards may produce better results than do monetary rewards and reinforcers.

Monetary bonuses, typically, do not provide the necessary "trophy effect" to symbolize that the individual or team has succeeded.

Therefore, in establishing positive consequences for individuals who meet or exceed what is expected of them, some consideration should be given to reinforcing individuals with non-monetary rewards, in addition to or, as an alternative to, monetary rewards, in order to provide the necessary "trophy effect" to symbolize the winning results.

Indeed, Bob Nelson discusses *1001 WAYS TO REWARD EMPLOYEES* in his best-selling book by the same name, many of which are in the form of non-monetary, rather than monetary rewards and reinforcers.

CONSEQUENCES MAY DIFFER

In terms of "Establishing Consequences," it also is important to appreciate that the types and degrees of consequences may differ, given the relationship of the parties.

For example, should a new employee fail to meet the requirements of the job, as previously defined for him or her at the time of hire, the consequence might be a separation from employment. Should a player fail to comply with a coach's rule, he or she might be "kicked off the team."

However, few parents are going to establish a consequence that if a child does not meet the expectations of the parents, he or she will be "kicked out of the home."

Therefore, it is essential that applicable consequences carefully be considered before being communicated to the other person in the relationship. The degree and nature of the consequence might vary with the importance and significance of the expectation. Likewise, the degree and nature of the consequence may differ due to the uniqueness of the relationship between the parties.

CONSEQUENCES
REQUIRE REITERATION

As with "Defining Expectations," it also may be beneficial periodically to reiterate and repeat what the negative consequences will be, if a given expectation is not met, as well as reinforcing what positive consequences will occur if the expectation is met.

Once "expectations" have been defined and "consequences" have been established, it then is necessary to train him or her on the specific tasks or behaviors necessary to meet such expectations. Exactly how this training and nurturing process should proceed is the substance of the "Third Secret to Perfect Coaching, Perfect Supervising, Perfect Parenting, and Building Successful and Lasting Relationships."

Remember
a failure to "Establish Consequences" creates a vacuum in the relationship, the result of which is likely to cause the relationship to be less successful, than otherwise.

3

The
Third
Secret

Coaches Encourage – Bosses Punish

3.
The Third Secret

P arental experts frequently explain that most children want to please their parents and, in most situations, will do everything possible to do so. Management gurus, likewise, exclaim that most new employees truly want to perform in accordance with the performance standards of the job they are assigned.

The same proposition applies to all types of relationships: the desire to please the other party to the relationship.

Therefore, once an employee, team member, student, child, friend, loved-one, or whomever is informed of what is expected and what consequences will apply for the failure to meet the expectation, a proper framework then is in place from which to launch the "Third Secret."

When training someone to perform or behave in a certain manner, the key is to "Encourage the Heart."

The "Third Secret" defines the process through which an individual can best be trained to meet whatever expectations are required of him or her.

The "Third Secret" dictates that the best approach in training and nurturing an individual to meet or exceed expectations is to focus on "Positive Reinforcement" instead of resorting to "Punitive Measures." In the words of the renowned co-author of the best selling book, the *ONE-MINUTE MANAGER* and other best selling publications and, an internationally acclaimed speaker, Ken Blanchard:

When training others, it is important to try to catch them doing something "right" instead of trying to catch them doing something "wrong."

The "Third Secret" consists of three profound words; that is, when training and nurturing others, the key is to: **ENCOURAGE THE HEART**.

As mentioned in the Preface of this book, there has been a paradigm shift in the American workplace during the past 30 years.

"Bosses of the Past" were trained to use punishment as a training technique. They were taught such buzz words as "shape-up or ship-out," "do not let the door hit you in the backside on your way out," or perhaps the most infamous, "my way or the highway."

Did the "punitive" approach to training employees ever work? Perhaps somewhat in years past, when employees responded more favorably to authoritarian figures.

But, in reality, the "punitive" approach to training was never an effective one.

PUNISHMENT DOES NOT WORK AS A TRAINING TECHNIQUE

Studies demonstrate that most employees come into the workplace in a most positive mindframe, hoping to be successful. Whether that positive attitude is sustained or not depends upon his or her supervisor's training technique.

When a supervisor uses "Positive Reinforcement" as a training enhancement, positive attitudes persist. When the supervisor uses punishment as a training method, the morale of such employees quickly deteriorates.

As a management consultant, throughout my career in working with all types of organizations to improve performance and employee morale, I have observed on countless occasions an unbelievable turnover rate of employees, principally, as a result of a punitive approach to training. Yet, executives, managers, and supervisors completely were unaware as to the reason for the turnover.

I, likewise, have observed all types of relationships fail as a result of a "punishment" mentality on the part of the trainer.

I continue to be amused at some parents' approach to teaching their children to drive a vehicle. The child typically knows little, if anything, regarding traffic laws, the appropriate method to use when parallel parking, or even how properly to engage and disengage the vehicle. Yet, I observe through the window of the vehicle, as well as hear, the parent screaming at the child about the manner the vehicle is being driven.

Certainly, if a child is driving in an unsafe manner as to create some danger, the parent would be more than justified in getting the child's attention. Typically, however, the screaming scenario is all too often the standard teaching method used by parents, whether an impending danger exists, or not.

No wonder so many children want to take "drivers training" from anyone in the world except from their parents.

I recently heard a caller on a radio "talk show" explain how his father would take him to the "woodshed" and beat him with a whip because he didn't make sufficient grades in school. That is, until on one occasion when he was older, he took the whip from his father and turned "the table," the consequence of which was to spend a few years in a correctional institution. He went on to explain about his learning disabilities and no matter how often or severe his father would beat him, he did not have the ability to make the grades his father expected.

The use of punishment as a training technique is not isolated to parents, managers, and spouses. Coaches, unfortunately, have been taught that punishment is appropriate when training players, as well.

Many years ago, long before I designed and developed the LOCKED-IN® GOLF SWING, I was practicing one day at a driving range when a well-known golf instructor approached me about taking some lessons from him. I reluctantly agreed.

Within moments of instructing me on a certain swing technique, he proceeded to scream and yell at me each time I attempted to swing the club, "YOU LISTEN TO ME AND YOU LISTEN TO ME NOW" and "YOU GET MY DRIFT" were his favorite expressions.

Finally, to his seemingly amazement, I inquired: "How much do I owe you up to now?" "Why?" he asked, appearing rather confused. I replied, "Because *this* golf lesson is over."

It not only is inappropriate to criticize during training, it equally is ineffective. "Punishment" as a training technique has never worked whether applied in the workplace, in the home, during "drivers training," or on the golf range.

Why?

"Punishment" as a training technique cannot work because the employee does not yet know how to behave or perform, the child does not know yet precisely how to behave or perform, and the player does not know yet specifically how to behave or perform while being trained.

It truly is ironic that parents use such generous doses of "Positive Reinforcement" when teaching and nurturing their babies to walk yet, when teaching and training the same children a few years later to achieve other tasks, they resort to "punishment."

It truly is enigmatic that a supervisor takes such delight when "encouraging" his or her toddler to speak those first few words, then proceeds to "punish" the newly hired employee over some procedure or task about which the new employee is unaware.

The use of punishment as a training technique also can cause confusion.

For example, a next door neighbor's dog started digging holes in the owner's backyard. The owner would beat the dog. Each time the owner would beat the dog, the dog would dig more holes.

Finally, in an exasperated state, the owner asked his neighbor, a psychologist, what in the world was wrong with his stupid dog. The psychologist remarked that it was apparent to him that the dog believed the reason he was being beaten was because he was not digging *enough* holes.

THE "PUNISHMENT" MENTALITY IS REPETITIVE

The "Boss of the Past" whether in the form of a supervisor, parent, coach, teacher, spouse, or whomever, was taught, programmed and conditioned to use "punishment" as a training technique. It became the model for others to follow.

The most damaging and troublesome consequence resulting from the use of "punishment" as a training technique is its replication. It becomes a repeated approach. Punishment becomes the standard by which to train others; then punishment begets more punishment in the next generation and in each subsequent generation.

If a child understands that punishment is an appropriate model to be used in training and nurturing children, the child may well, in turn, use punishment as a standard in training and nurturing his or her own children.

If a child observes a parent physically abusing the other parent in an attempt to teach the abused parent who's "in charge," the child may well accept such punitive measure as an acceptable one and, in turn, later abuse his or her own spouse for the same purpose.

If an employee observes the use of punishment as a training technique in the workplace and later is promoted to a management position, he or she may well believe that the use of punitive measures during the training process is not only an acceptable approach but, perhaps, a preferred approach.

It is so human to emulate; it is so natural to accept the long-held notion that the answer to developing others is to punish them.

It is time for this fixation to punish others as a teaching technique to end. It is time for the use of punishment in an attempt to train, develop and control others to stop.

WHAT REALLY WORKS WHEN TRAINING OTHERS

The most effective technique to use when training others is to establish a proper foundation for the process; that is, defining the expectations desired and establishing the positive consequences if such expectations are met.

In other words, the "First and Second Secrets" provide the platform and foundation to begin the training phase. "Defining Expectations and Establishing Consequences" provide an appropriate environment by and through which the person being trained can be motivated to succeed.

Then, by merely supplying ample "encouragement" and generous doses of "positive reinforcement" during the training curve, the training results practically are guaranteed.

There are several factors to consider when using the power of "Positive Reinforcement" as a training technique.

FIRST FACTOR

The first factor to consider in the process of "Positive Reinforcement" training is: Praise for incremental successes, however small, rather than reserve encouragement only for significant achievements.

Most "Defined Expectations" consist of multiple steps or processes – whether such expectations apply to employees, children, team members, or whomever. Managers, parents, coaches, and others who train, therefore, should reinforce "small successes" that relate to the satisfactory completion of each task or step, rather than wait until the satisfactory completion of all the tasks and steps.

For example, given my frequent travels as a professional speaker and consultant, a few years ago my wife wanted to find a Shetland dog as a pet. She was successful in finding a beautiful Sheltie "show dog," that, for whatever reason, did not work out all that well in show business. My wife named the dog, "Dallas."

Dallas would have nothing to do with anyone, including myself, except for my wife. The dog would not come near me which was somewhat disturbing when my friends would remark: "Dogs always can detect the worst in people."

Then it became a challenge. I was going to bond with Dallas somehow. I began to lay "bacon bits" approximately ten or fifteen feet in front of me. While I was not observing, Dallas would gingerly "sneak-up" on the "bacon bits" and consume them.

Day-by-day, I would leave the bacon bits nearer my favorite chair. He slowly began to come closer until, eventually, he would eat from my hand.

Nowadays, Dallas will not leave my side. We have bonded – all by a process of taking incremental steps with the "bacon bits" until the ultimate expectation was met.

SECOND FACTOR

Another factor to appreciate in the "Third Secret" is that reinforcing positive behavior should not cease just because the training process is completed.

The degree of encouraging and positively reinforcing an individual who has mastered the expectations may be less frequent in comparison with the initial training and nurturing period. Nonetheless, applying "positive reinforcement" is a continuing and timeless process; indeed, a "forever" process.

The continuation of the use of "encouragement" and "positive reinforcement" after the training process is completed creates an opportunity to empower.

Once a child has mastered what a parent expects, the child becomes empowered to manage himself or herself with respect to the performance of such task. Equally, when an employee completes the training period and has mastered certain skills as-

"Self-Management" means that individuals who have mastered the expectations are, in turn, empowered to manage themselves.

sociated with the performance requirements of a given job, he or she then becomes empowered to improve upon those skills.

THE MAGIC OF
SELF-MANAGEMENT

Once an employee, team member, or child is able to master all the functions associated with what is expected, he or she then will have the ability to become a "Self-Manager."

"Self-Management" is the process of training an individual through the first "Three Secrets" in such a manner that, in turn, the individual will know more about the tasks and skills associated with the expectations than anyone else; he or she will know more about the significance of the expectations than anyone else; he or she will know more how to perform the tasks and skills associated with the expectations than anyone else; and, in turn, he or she can better manage himself or herself than can anyone else.

"Self-Management" means that individuals who have mastered the expectations are, in turn, empowered to manage themselves.

When "Self-Management" occurs, the role of the person defining the expectation is elevated from that of one who trains to that of one who provides resources to the individual who has become his or her own "Self-Manager."

This transformation from the "trainer" to "resourcer" completes the empowerment loop in that the ultimate role of the coach is to provide the necessary resources to ensure all members of the team are winners. The same transformation holds true in all types of relationships: the parent is elevated from a "trainer" of the child to a "resourcer" for the child; the teacher is elevated from a "teacher" of the student to a "resourcer" for the student; and the supervisor is elevated from a "trainer" of the new employee to a "resourcer" for the employee.

RAISING THE "BAR" OF EXPECTATIONS

Another factor associated with the "Third Secret" is to appreciate the importance of periodically raising the levels of expectations and, of course, the corresponding levels of rewards and reinforcers, when the initial levels of expectations are met, or exceeded.

Human nature requires that the human spirit continually be challenged to higher levels of expectations in order to provide a basis for continuing motivation.

"TRAINING DEFICIENCY" VERSUS "ATTITUDINAL DEFICIENCY"

A most challenging dilemma occurs when, after sufficient training through the use of positive reinforcement, the person being trained fails to meet the "Defined Expectations."

There are several reasons why an individual may fail to meet the "expectations" defined for her or him during the training and nurturing process.

First, maybe the "expectations" were not sufficiently and clearly defined. In such case, a renewed effort may be necessary to ensure the expectations are more meticulously explained.

Second, perhaps the "consequences" were not sufficiently and clearly established so that the person being trained adequately understood their significance. If so, it may be important to re-establish the positive consequences of meeting the expectations.

Human nature requires that the human spirit continually be challenged to higher levels of expectations in order to provide a basis for continuing motivation.

Thirdly, maybe the person being trained does not have the "desire" to meet or exceed the expectations. In such circumstances, a re-emphasized effort should be made to impress upon the person being trained of the negative consequences that will apply if expectations are not met.

Perhaps the individual being trained was misjudged in the first place and does not have the ability to meet the "Defined Expectations," in which case, a "tough decision" sometimes is necessary in terms of removing the individual from such dilemma.

Lastly, it may be that the individual previously has demonstrated that he or she can meet the expectations but no longer desires to do so. Therefore, it is most important that parents, coaches, teachers, managers, and others in leadership positions recognize the distinction between a "training deficiency" and an "attitudinal deficiency."

Sometimes, whenever an individual is failing to meet the defined expectations during training, the failure is what might be characterized as a "training deficiency," in which case it is necessary to start the first "Three Secrets" anew: **Re-define Expectations, Re-establish Consequences and**

If an individual's failure to meet the expectations during the training process is a "result of a lack of training," then it will be necessary to start the process anew.

Continue to Encourage the Heart by Using Positive Re-inforcement.

On the other hand, sometimes the failure to meet the expectations during the training and nurturing process may be a result of an attitude, rather than a result of a lack of training. If the person being trained has shown that he or she can meet the defined expectations, the failure, thereafter, to continue to meet the expectations certainly is one of an attitude rather than a result of a lack of training.

Unfortunately, even with the very best of team members, employees, children, or whomever, "attitudinal" behaviors arise.

As unpleasant a task as it may be, if the failure of the individual to continue to meet the defined expectations is a result of an "attitude," it is necessary to apply the "Fourth Secret to Perfect Coaching, Perfect Supervising, Perfect Parenting, and Building Successful and Lasting Relationships."

<u>Remember</u>
The failure to "Encourage the Heart" during the training process leaves a vacuum in the relationship, the result of which is likely to cause the relationship to be less successful than otherwise.

4

The
Fourth
Secret

Coaches Encourage – Bosses Punish

4.
The Fourth Secret

The "Fourth Secret" addresses the situation in which an individual has been trained to meet the "Defined Expectations," but then fails or refuses to continue to perform or behave in accordance with what is expected. It addresses what to do with an "attitudinal deficiency."

A failure to address an "attitudinal deficiency" compromises the integrity of the "Defined Expectations," and thus is not an option. To address an "attitudinal deficiency" in an improper manner polarizes the individual into a further "negative attitude" which, likewise, compromises the integrity of the expectations; and, again, is not an effective option.

The "Fourth Secret," therefore must provide a corrective process that results in the matter being addressed without worsening the situation.

When criticizing another, if the intent is to hurt the other person, do not do it. If you do, it will come back at you ten fold.

The "Fourth Secret to Perfect Coaching, Perfect Supervising, Perfect Parenting, and Building Successful and Lasting Relationships" is:

"Attack The Behavior – Not The Person"

When addressing an "attitudinal deficiency," it is essential to attack the behavior of the individual, rather than his or her "person." It is important to separate the behavior *of* the individual *from* the individual and focus and concentrate on the behavior, rather than on the person.

Most people do not resent their behaviors being attacked, typically, as long as they are approached in a courteous and positive way. Most people substantially resent being attacked on a personal level. Not only is the individual subject to the personal attack hurt, so is the person directing the attack.

To paraphrase Napoleon Hill, author of the book, THINK AND GROW RICH: when criticizing another, if the intent is to hurt the other person, do not do it. If you do, it will come back at you ten fold.

The intent must be to help the person being criticized; not to hurt him or her.

USE "CORRECTIVE" RATHER THAN "PUNITIVE" ACTION WHEN ADDRESSING AN "ATTITUDINAL DEFICIENCY"

The "Fourth Secret" merely is an extension of the "Second Secret": establishing negative consequences in the event the individual fails to meet the expectations. It is the application of the previously "Established Consequence."

If a child, employee, student, player, or whomever, previously has been informed of the consequences in the event the expectations are not met, then there should be no surprise when the consequences are invoked and applied.

THE ESTABLISHMENT AND APPLICATION OF THE CONSEQUENCE MUST CORRESPOND

The application of the consequence to address a given "attitudinal deficiency" must conform to its antecedent, the initial establishment of the consequence.

For example, the consequence that might be applied to a failure of an employee to continue to meet the organization's expectations could be a termination of employment. However, the employee should have been informed, or should have known in some way, that his or her omission or commission of performance or behavior would result in dismissal.

The consequence that might be applied for the failure of a child to meet an expectation may differ from an action taken against an employee, because the relationship is different. Whatever the consequence applied, it should agree with what was established in the beginning. The same holds true for all types of relationships.

PUNISHMENT IS NOT AN EFFECTIVE SOLUTION TO ADDRESS "ATTITUDINAL DEFICIENCIES"

Just as punishment is inappropriate to use during the training process, punishment likewise is inappropriate to use when addressing a child, employee, player, or whomever, who has demonstrated and shown that he or she can meet the expectations, but chooses no longer to do so.

If punishment is not appropriate to use to address an "attitudinal deficiency," then how do you ensure accountability? How is it possible to make a child accountable for his or her behavior without the use of punishment? How do you ensure employee accountability without using punishment?

There is a quantum distinction between using "punitive measures" in an effort to ensure accountability and using "corrective measures" to ensure others are accountable for their behaviors.

I define punishment as attacking another on a personal level by making the "person" the topic of discussion, rather than that of the "behavior" of the person.

The most appropriate and effective approach in addressing the failure of another to meet an expectation is to separate the "behavior" from the person and concentrate on the "behavior."

This approach is the essence of the "Fourth Secret." It is the distinction between an approach "to punish" and an approach "to correct."

Too often, parents have been programmed and conditioned not only to use punishment as a means to teach their children during the training period, given a specific expectation, but to continue to punish as a means to resolve an "attitudinal deficiency."

This same propensity to punish as a means to address "attitudinal deficiencies" equally occurs in the classroom , on the playground and in the workplace. Particularly is the predisposition "to punish" instead of "to correct" prevalent in the workplace.

For example, most organizations provide a progressive disciplinary procedure to address violations of rules and policies. Except for "dischargeable" infractions in the first instance, such as theft, gross insubordination, etc., less serious offenses typically are processed through a sequence of reprimands, the last of which provides for discharge.

Effective managers, supervisors and leaders in the workplace approach this progressive disciplinary process in a "corrective" manner. They attack the behavior of the employee, instead of his or her person. Unfortunately, there yet are too many managers, supervisors, and leaders in the workplace who approach the progressive disciplinary process as an opportunity "to punish" by attacking the employee in a personal way, rather than "to correct" the behavior in a professional manner.

Employees, not unlike children and others with whom we have relationships, possess a predisposition to become very hostile and defensive when they are attacked personally. Such reaction is a function of the human spirit to protect and defend oneself.

Many organizations provide suspensions in their progressive disciplinary procedure prior to the discharge stage. I always have taken exception to the use of suspensions as part of an organization's progressive disciplinary process, prior to the discharge stage, because of its "punitive" implications.

But, admittedly, I am biased on this issue, given what happened to me in the fourth grade of elementary school. Frankly, I was "expelled." I was "expelled" for one day – for throwing paper wads across the classroom.

I will never forget *that* long walk home to face my mother at 10:00 o'clock that morning. "What are you doing home at 10:00 o'clock in the morning? I thought you were at school," she inquired.

I got "expelled," I replied.

For generations, no one in my family had ever been expelled from school. Even to this day, decades later, some less diplomatic members of my family cannot refrain from bringing my fourth grade indiscretion to everyones' attention – at family retreats, at holiday gatherings and even on Mother's Day.

Can you imagine a 45 year old employee, suspended from work, driving home at 10:00 a.m. in the summertime to face his children, playing on the front lawn.

"What are you doing home at 10:00 o'clock in the morning, Daddy; we thought you were at work," they inquire. The answer; "I got expelled."

Believe me, any employee in the workplace who ever has been suspended from work and any kid who has ever been expelled from school will tell you in no uncertain terms that being suspended is "punishment"; getting expelled is a "stigma."

When I speak of a suspension from work as part of a final warning, I am discussing an interim phase of corrective action, rather than a final disposition of the matter.

Therefore, I recommend to organizations whom I counsel to appreciate the distinction between a progressive "corrective" action, prior to the discharge step, and the discharge step itself.

Specifically, I recommend that prior to the termination stage in a progressive disciplinary process, it is the "behavior" of the employee that should be addressed.

What then is the alternative to a suspension as part of a final warning in a progressive disciplinary process, if not suspension? The alternative is to place the employee on what some organizations characterize as a "conditional status."

The employee is informed as a part of a final warning, that rather than a suspension, he or she will be placed on "conditional status." The employee is advised that a certain number of conditions must be met within a given time period. If such conditions are met within the specified time period, the employee will be permitted to remain employed with the organization. If not, he or she will have two choices: resign or be terminated from employment.

One might add an additional caveat: "If you have no intention of meeting these conditions, please respect the organization and yourself and do the 'right thing.' Please resign because we do not want to be placed in a position at the end of the time period to have to discharge you."

Many organizations do not have the flexibility or discretion for a "conditional status" approach because of a labor agreement that provides otherwise. Other organizations are less creative because the decision makers in the organization are so entrenched in a "punishment" mentality that they are blind to the concept of "correcting." They argue that a suspension creates a much stronger impact on an employee than does "conditional status." True. Such a strong impact that it polarizes the employee against the organization to such a degree the organization might be better served to have terminated the employee instead of having suspended him or her in the first place.

On the other hand, when an employee is placed on "conditional status," the matter can be handled in a very confidential and private manner, in contrast to being embarrassed and humiliated in front of co-workers. Equally significant, the ownership of whether or not the employee continues in the relationship with the organization remains with the employee.

It is so important to distinguish an interim stage of corrective action from the stage of last resort.

Whether it is an employee, student, child, player, or someone else in a relationship, the "corrective" approach rather than the "punitive" approach should be the standard applied to address "attitudinal deficiencies" up to the point that other more drastic measures must be applied as a "final" disposition.

Before a team member is "kicked off the team," for some minor infraction, a "corrective approach" first should be exhausted to resolve the behavior. Prior to suspending a child from a classroom, the teacher should exhaust "corrective" avenues to resolve the behavior, except for behaviors that are so disruptive there is no other feasible alternative.

And, God forbid, before a child is "kicked out of the home" in keeping with the provisions of a "tough love" contract, the parents should more than exhaust alternative solutions in a "corrective" spirit.

Whether correcting the behavior of a player, a student, a child, an employee, or whomever, there are several steps an individual may take to ensure that the focus is on the "behavior" of the person being counseled or reprimanded, rather than on his or her "person."

The 12 Steps to Corrective Action are:

1. Get All The Facts

It is important to gather all the pertinent and material facts prior to drawing some premature conclusion relative to another's behavior. For example, maybe an employee is out of his work area and the manager to whom he or she reports "jumps" to the conclusion that the employee should be counseled about the matter; even officially reprimanded, only to find out, too late, that the employee was in the other work area at the direction of the general manager as a result of an emergency.

2. Be Consistent With Previous Practice

To the extent possible, it is important to be consistent with past precedent when counseling or reprimanding another. When corrective action is applied differently and inconsistent with the type or degree of previous corrective action, it creates confusion and resentment, cries of favoritism and discrimination, whether such action applies to a child, employee, student, team player, or whomever.

Certainly, in today's workplace, each and every disciplinary action might result in some type of charge of discrimination or employee lawsuit. Most such complaints and lawsuits are won or lost on the basis of consistency; consistency in terms of addressing behaviors in keeping with defined expectations and established consequences, and consistency in terms of adhering to past practice and precedent within and throughout all departments and shifts within a local organization.

3. Plan Ahead And Mentally Role Play Exactly How The Corrective Action Will Be Addressed

Whether parent, coach, supervisor, teacher or, whomever, it is most important that such individual who is about to engage in an interaction with the child, player, employee, student, or whomever, plan out exactly when, where and how the interaction will take place and what exactly is to be discussed with such individual who has failed to meet the expectations.

4. Reprimand In Private

Remember the old adage: "praise in public; reprimand in private."

An individual may reserve the most private place, imaginable, to address a disciplinary matter. Yet, it may not appear to be very private if the person to be reprimanded is "called out" in front of his or her peers and then escorted to the "private place."

Everything an individual does in terms of actions and deeds will be interpreted by the person being reprimanded or counseled as either "corrective" or "punitive."

5. Avoid Distractions And Interruptions When Counseling And Reprimanding

The person reprimanding another should not only ensure that such reprimand takes place in private, but also that he or she will not be interrupted or distracted during the process.

Being interrupted by telephone calls or intrusions by others undermines the impact of the discussion and the respect one should maintain for the individual being corrected.

6. Be Specific When Describing The Reason For The Corrective Session

Managers, parents, teachers, coaches, and others, should inform those they are reprimanding as to the specifics surrounding their investigation: specifics in terms of what has been investigated, in what manner the investigation was conducted, the conclusions of the investigation, and so on. It is inappropriate to play the guessing game when reprimanding another. For example, consider this scenario. The supervisor inquires of the employee: "guess why we are having this discussion?" The employee responds: "Because of so and so?" The supervisor replies: "I wasn't even aware you did that!" Now there are two situations to address instead of one. Be specific when reprimanding!

7. Solicit The Other "Side Of The Story"

As Stephen Covey, the "7-Habits" guru, suggests: *seek first to understand*; a very fundamental principle to apply when reprimanding or counseling children. Also, it is a most sound principle to apply when reprimanding or counseling a team member, employee, student, or whomever.

The individual may have had a good and mitigating reason for his or her behavior. On the other hand, his or her explanation possibly could worsen the situation for the individual. One doesn't know until such an inquiry is made.

8. Determine Whether The Behavior Dictates An Application Of Assistance And Rehabilitation Or Whether The Behavior Dictates An Application Of Corrective Discipline

Does the behavior of the individual "call" for assistance or does the behavior of the individual "call" for a reprimand?

The best test to determine whether to apply "assistance" or to apply "discipline" is to answer this question: is the behavior beyond the control of the individual or is the behavior within the control of the individual? Usually, whenever the behavior of the individual is beyond the control of the individual (such as alcoholism), the approach would be to apply assistance. On the other hand, if the behavior of the individual is within the control of the person, but, yet, he or she elects not to control the behavior (such as insubordination), the approach would be to apply "corrective" discipline.

9. Transfer The Behavior Of The Individual Back To The Person Being Counseled Or Reprimanded

Never permit an employee, team member, student, child, or anyone to transfer the ownership of a behavior to the one conducting the reprimand.

Most employees, team members, students, and children attempt to remove themselves from the ownership of their behaviors by transferring the ownership of their behaviors to their managers, teachers, coaches, or parents.

In order to ensure that the person being counseled or reprimanded accepts ownership of his or her behavior, it is necessary to transfer the individual's behavior back to him or her; better yet, never permit it to be transferred away from the person being reprimanded in the first place.

10. Get A Commitment From The Person Being Reprimanded Or Counseled

The best way to transfer the ownership of a behavior back to the individual engaging in the behavior is to elicit a commitment from such person as to what steps he or she is willing to take in order to accept responsibility for correcting the behavior.

With respect to employees, even a written commitment statement by the employee as to what steps he or she will be taking to correct the behavior may be an effective approach.

With respect to children, players, students, and others, etc., a verbal commitment can serve this purpose.

11. Document The Behavior Of The Person Being Counseled Or Reprimanded

Without documentation, it becomes an employee's word against the word of a manager should the behavior and the corrective action be at issue in some subsequent legal proceeding. With documentation, the manager at least has a "fighting chance" to substantiate what took place with the corrective action.

Obviously, in terms of relationships outside the workplace, formal written documentation may appear overly reactive. Mental recordation may be in order, with respect to players, children, and others outside the workplace.

12. Conclude The Corrective Session In A Positive Manner

It is important to end the corrective discussion on a positive note; again, by focusing on the behavior of the individual rather than focusing on him or her as a person.

The message essentially should communicate that "you're OK, I'm OK, everybody's OK as a person; it's not you as a person that is at issue, it is your behavior."

Therefore, when the child, employee, student, player, or whomever, walks away from the corrective interaction, he or she will focus on the behavior, rather than be upset about being attacked personally.

By simply applying these 12 positive steps to each and every disciplinary situation, the manager, coach, teacher and the parent can ensure that the employee, team member, student and child will conclude that his or her behavior was the focus of the reprimand or counseling, not him or her as a person.

What if the "corrective steps" do not resolve the "attitudinal deficiency" of the respective child, employee, student, player, or whomever? What then?

When the "Four Secrets" properly are applied, including the 12 corrective steps discussed above, there should be few, if any, "attitudinal deficiencies" that persist to the extent that a final disposition of last resort must be applied.

In the rare event, however, that an employee must be terminated from employment, a student must be removed from a given school, or a child must find some other place to reside outside the home, I suggest that "punishment" does not have to be the focus of such decision.

The employee chose to terminate himself or herself from employment by a refusal or failure to comply with the final conditions imposed to salvage the relationship. The player "kicked himself or herself off the team" by a failure to play by the rules of the game and by the rules established by the coach. The child removed himself or herself from the home by a failure to honor the "final" conditions established by the parents in the "tough love" contract.

No one was punished. They merely were victims of their own behavior. They exercised the behavior; not the manager, teacher, coach, or parent.

Therefore, I am convinced that even a final disposition to address "attitudinal deficiencies" can be accomplished in a "corrective" manner by addressing the "behavior," rather than in a "punitive" manner, by addressing the "person."

I have observed during my career that some managers and supervisors had the "gift of correctness" sufficient to discharge an employee in such a corrective manner that the employee would shake the managers hand at the end of the termination session, thank the supervisor for the opportunity to have worked with him or her, go home and send a special "thank you" note to the company as well as a letter to the editor of the local newspaper about what a wonderful supervisor he or she had while working for the company.

On the other hand, I have observed some managers with such a "punishment" mentality during the discharge session, that the employee figuratively would take a piece of furniture and attack the supervisor, go home and get a shotgun, return back to the facility and "blast" the supervisor away.

What's the distinction?

The first manager addressed the "behavior" of the employee being terminated; the latter manager attacked the "person" of the employee being terminated.

Remember

Attacking a person, rather than a behavior, creates hostility on the part of the recipient, the consequence of which is likely to cause the relationship to be less successful than otherwise.

Even during the last and final stage of a relationship, the approach nonetheless can be corrective rather than punitive – simply by separating the "behavior" from the "person" in the discussion – and "ATTACKING THE BEHAVIOR – NOT THE PERSON."

The good news is, when the first "Three Secrets" are applied, in the vast majority of cases, the "Fourth Secret" will never be at issue.

The equally good news is, even when the "Fourth Secret" has to be applied, effective relationships, nonetheless, can be maintained.

Remember, Too, a failure to apply any of the Four Secrets carves a hole so deep into the soul of the relationship, the relationship is doomed from the beginning.

Epilogue

The essence of *COACHES ENCOURAGE – BOSSES PUNISH* is found in the "Third Secret"; that is, to "Encourage the Heart."

Although the other secrets are necessary in order for the "Third Secret" to function, reinforcing positive behavior is the "HEART AND SOUL" to building effective and enduring relationships.

As parents, it is so important that we never give up on our children. We may be the last and only hope that a child has left. We always must continue to encourage and reinforce positive behaviors of our children, irrespective of age or station in life. Parents who lose contact with their children, who disconnect from their children and who no longer relate to their children are missing a most significant part of the journey of life.

As parents, it is so
important that we
never give up on
our children. We
may be the last and
only hope
that a child has
left. We must
continue to provide
the "Gift of
Encouragement."

I recently heard a minister share a story about some parents who frequently complained about spending so much money on behalf of their daughter – clothes, car, college, wedding and so on.

The minister saw the couple a few years later. The father remarked to the minister, through the tears flowing down his cheeks, that they no longer were having to spend any money on their daughter. "She died two years ago in an automobile accident."

As managers, supervisors and leaders in the workplace, it is so essential to encourage and reinforce the positive behavior of employees, whether on the first day on the job or on the day of retirement.

As teachers and coaches, it is significant that we catch our students and players doing something "right," during training, and praise them, rather than attempting to catch them doing something "wrong" and criticizing them. Students and players, too, need an ample supply of "encouragement" and "positive reinforcement" because we, as teachers and coaches, may provide the last "ray of hope" that a given student or player has left.

Providing the "Gift Of Encouragement" and supplying the "Power Of Positive Reinforcement" is not limited to children, employees or players; they are necessary to the success of all meaningful and lasting relationships.

The 30 year era during which the American workplace, American family and the American conscience has transformed from the "Punisher of the Past" to the "Encourager of the Future" may well mark the defining moment in history of society's transcendence into a higher human dimension. The transformation from the "Boss of the Past" to the "Coach of the Future" hopefully will elevate all types of relationships into a more meaningful and significant human condition.

COACHES ENCOURAGE – BOSSES PUNISH is dedicated to this transformation.

Gordon Jackson

About The Author

GORDON JACKSON is an author, speaker, consultant and counselor on **Positive Employee Relations** and **Interactional Behaviors**.

As a speaker, he is a Who's Who in Professional Speaking and a Professional Member of the National Speakers Association. He is a "CSP" (Certified Speaking Professional), the highest accreditation awarded by the National Speakers Association.

He was featured as one of 31 Consummate Speakers for 1996 by participating Speakers Bureau in SHARING IDEAS, the international news magazine for speakers, meeting planners, and speakers bureaus.

As a consultant and counselor, he is the author of *THE LABOR AND EMPLOYMENT LAW DESK BOOK*, a one-volume manual on federal and state employment laws, *UNLAWFUL TERMINATIONS AND EMPLOYMENT-AT-WILL* and other employment related publications.

As an avid golfer, he is the author of the *LOCKED-IN®️ GOLF SWING*, an instructional book designed and developed for "Golfers who are too embarrassed to play but who love the game too much to quit."

Gordon Jackson averages in excess of 100 keynote addresses, banquet speeches, seminars and workshops annually, on such topics as:

*   **Management 2000** — Six Steps To Maintaining A "Trouble-Free" Workplace In The New Millennium

*   **Teams Without Tears** — Pitfalls To Avoid When Implementing Empowered Work Teams

*   **Profiles of Leadership** — Ten Leadership Lessons From Legendary Leaders

*   **Coaches Encourage – Bosses Punish** — Four Secrets To Perfect Coaching, Perfect Supervising, Perfect Parenting And Building Successful And Lasting Relationships

*   **How To Motivate People** — Magical Management Methods To Motivate In The New Millennium

*   **The Paradigm Golf Swing** — How "Paradigm Flexibility" Was Used In Designing, Developing And Mastering The **Locked-In® Golf Swing**

*For more information about
Gordon Jackson's Presentations, contact:*

Professional Resources Center, Inc.
P. O. Box 382036
Memphis, TN 38183-2036
Phone (901) 754-9404 • Fax (901) 756-4237

Order additional books for friends, family and co-workers
using the order form below.

Coaches Encourage – Bosses Punish

☐ *Enclosed is a check or money order for $* _____

☐ *Bill my firm. Purchase Order #* _____

Name _____ Date _____

Title _____ Day Phone _____

Company _____

Street Address _____

City _____ State _____ Zip _____

COACHES ENCOURAGE BOSSES PUNISH

Price	Qty	Amount
1-24	$10.95	_____
25-99	$9.95	_____
100 or more	$8.95	_____

Sub Total _____

▲ ▲ ▲ ▲ S/H _____

▲ TOTAL _____

SHIPPING & HANDLING	
Up to $50	$3.00
$50 - $99	$6.00
$100 - $500	$9.00
$500 or more	$12.00

Three Convenient Ways To Order:

- Phone order to 800 754-9404
  901 754-9404

- Fax order to 901 756-4237

- Mail this completed form to:
  Professional Resources Center, Inc.
  PO Box 382036
  Memphis, TN 38183-2036

Make checks payable to Professional Resources Center, Inc.